Outside-in

A lift-the-flap body book

Clare Smallman
with illustrations by Edwina Riddell

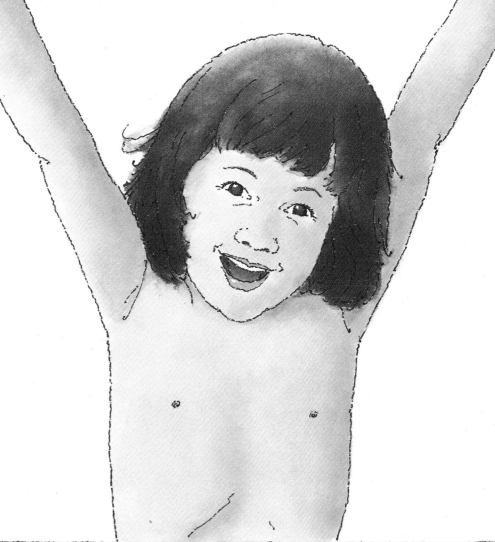

Macdonald

Skin all over

Your skin is very thin but very tough. Some people have black skin, some have brown and some have pink skin.

Skin has folds and is stretchy like elastic. It keeps your insides in and germs and water out. Look at the folds of skin in the palm of your hand.

All skin has oil in it. Your hands and feet don't have so much oil, so when you stay in the water they go wrinkly.

Lift the flap and see your muscles. Muscles pull your skin and bones about so you can move around.

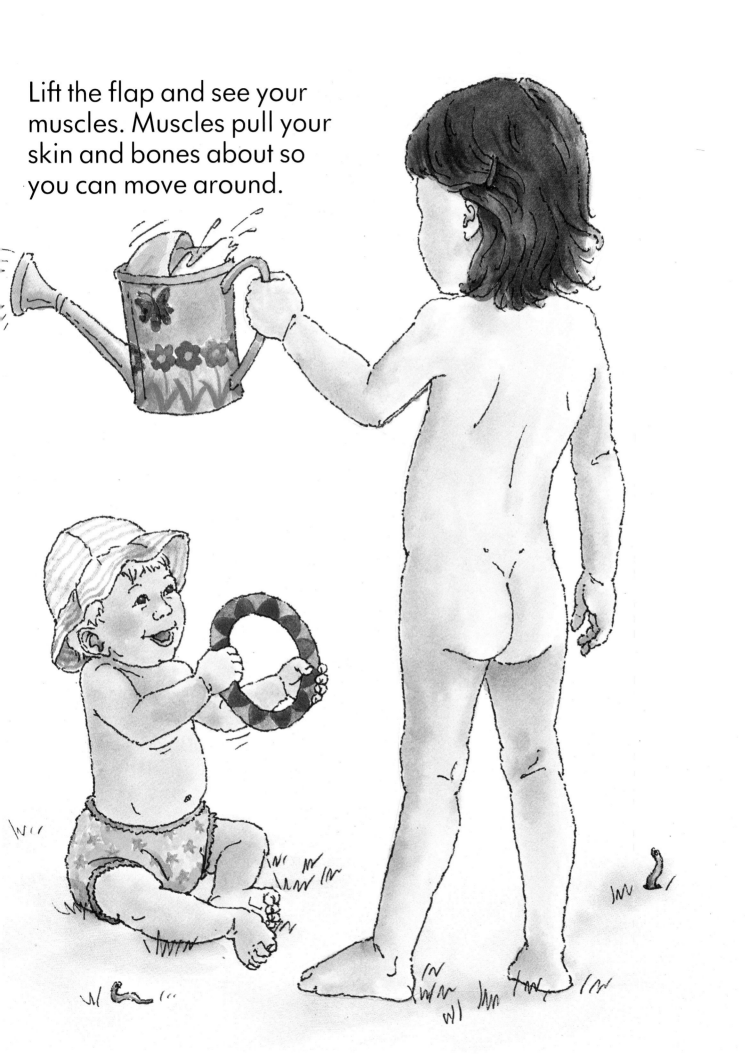

Keeping cool

When you feel hot your body makes wet sweat to cool you down. Put a little water on one arm and let it dry: which arm feels cooler?

Stroke the back of your arm and feel the short hairs. When you are hot the hairs lie flat and sweat leaks through the tiny holes in your skin to cool it. What else can you do to keep cool?

Keeping warm

When you are cold the little hairs on your skin stand up to try and trap warm air to keep you warm.

Can you see the little bird fluffing up its feathers to keep warm?
Scarves and clothes and gloves are even better at trapping air to keep you warm.

Breathing

You suck air in and blow it out all day and all night. That's breathing. Watch your chest move as you breathe.

Fresh air rushes in through your nose or mouth when your chest moves out. Air goes down your windpipe to lungs in your chest.

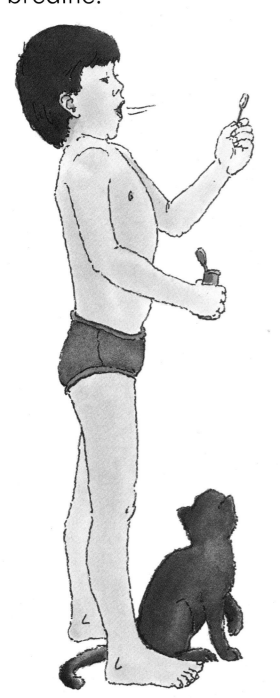

There is a flap in the windpipe and when you eat, it shuts to stop food going down to your lungs.

Your lungs are in a cage of ribs. How big do you think they are? Open the rib cage to find out.

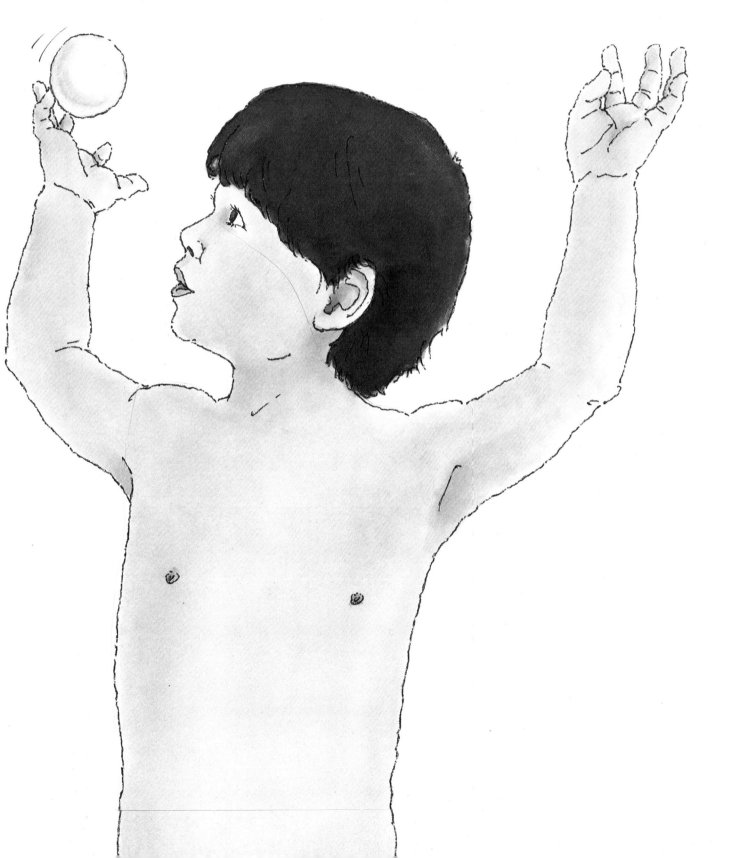

Inside your lungs

When your ribs move out they pull your lungs with them so they open up to their fullest and suck in air. When your ribs move in they squash the air out of your lungs.

It's like pushing air out of a balloon pump. Find out how much air you breathe by pretending to be a balloon pump. How much can you blow up a balloon with one breath?

You breathe out used air and breathe in fresh air. The useful part of fresh air is called oxygen. When you run or jump you need lots of it, and you have to breathe more quickly to get enough oxygen. When you stay still you can breathe slowly because you need less oxygen. When do you think you breathe slowest?

Bones and teeth

You have lots of bones in your body. Together they are called the skeleton. Lift the flap to see all the bones.

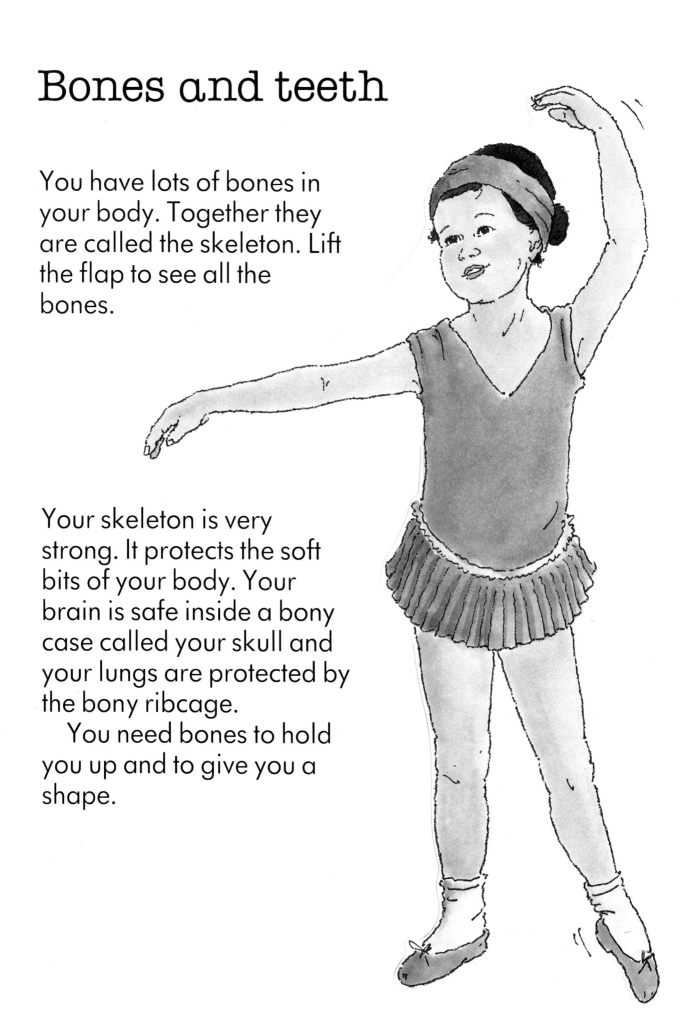

Your skeleton is very strong. It protects the soft bits of your body. Your brain is safe inside a bony case called your skull and your lungs are protected by the bony ribcage.

You need bones to hold you up and to give you a shape.

What shape do you think you would be without a skeleton to hold you up?

Teeth are the part of your skeleton that you can see. Like all your bony bits they are alive and growing and do well when you drink plenty of milk.

Teeth need more cleaning and looking after than the rest of your skeleton because they are on the outside.

Smallest and biggest

Your smallest bones are
tiny ones in your ear.
The thigh bone is your
biggest bone. Is your
thigh bone longer
than the one in
the picture?

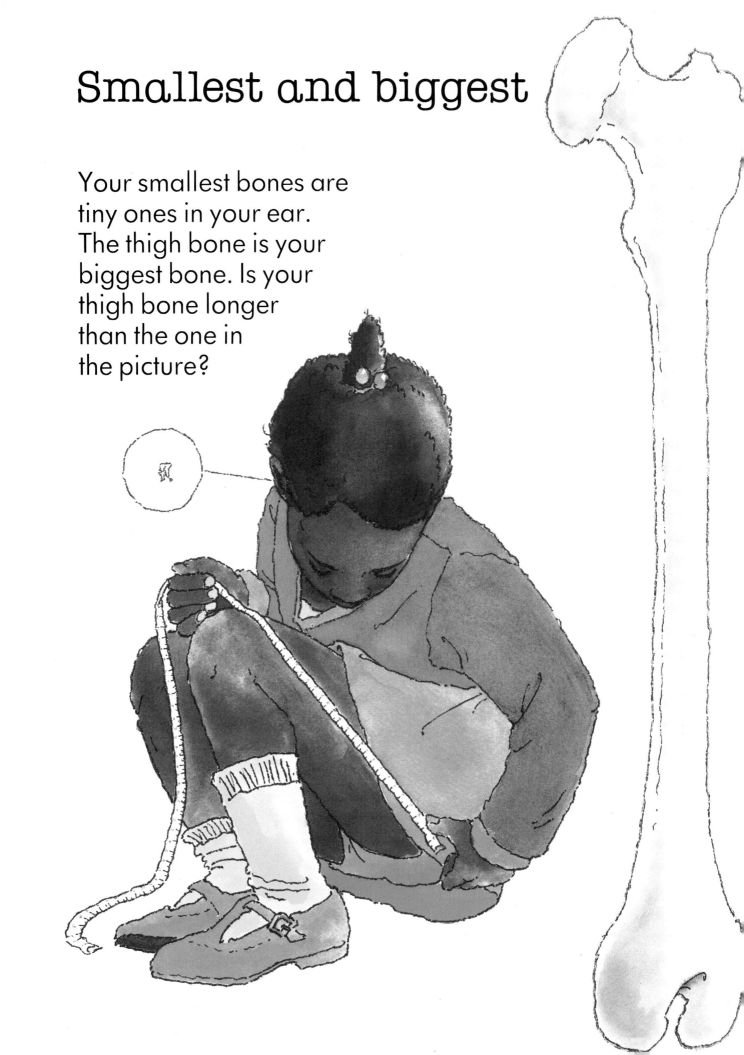

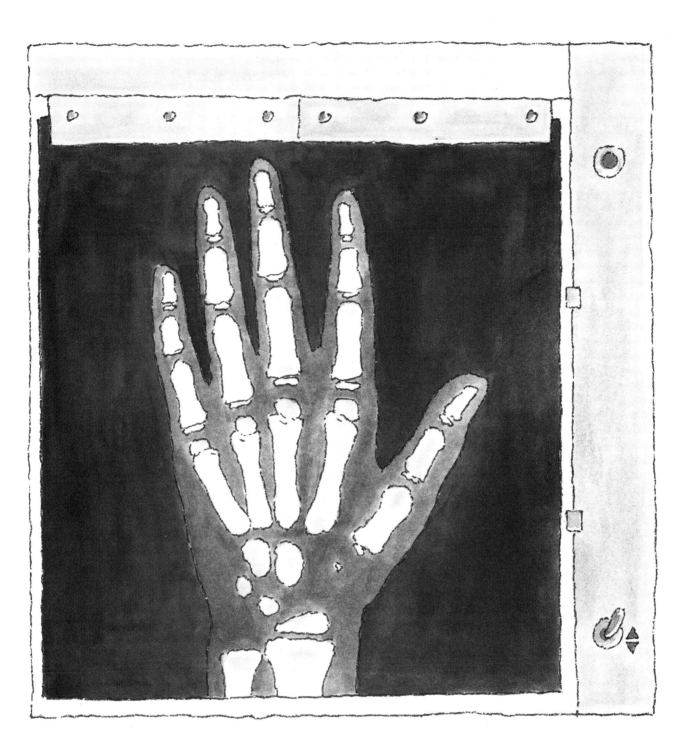

An X-ray picture shows the bones inside you. Joints are where bones meet. They let you bend. Your wrist joints let your hands bend to and fro like a door.

Skin and muscle and blood all look grey on an X-ray and bones look whiter. Is your hand bigger or smaller than the one in the X-ray picture?

What happens to your food?

All the food you eat is mixed up inside you. Your body has to sort out the useful bits.

Food travels through a long tube while it is sorted. The journey begins when you chew food and mix it with spit. That makes it easier to swallow.

Your food tube is made of muscles. The muscles push the food down along the tube. It's like squeezing a tube of toothpaste. Sometimes the muscles push the wrong way and you throw up.

Does the apple go to her head, to her arms or straight down the middle? Lift the flap and see.

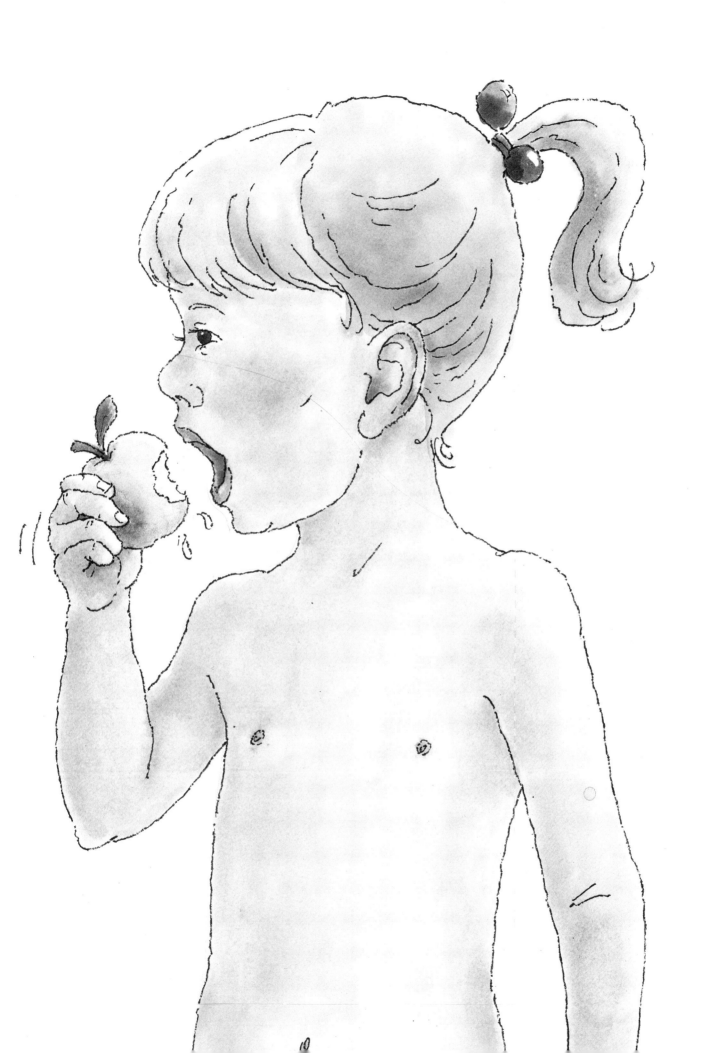

The journey goes on

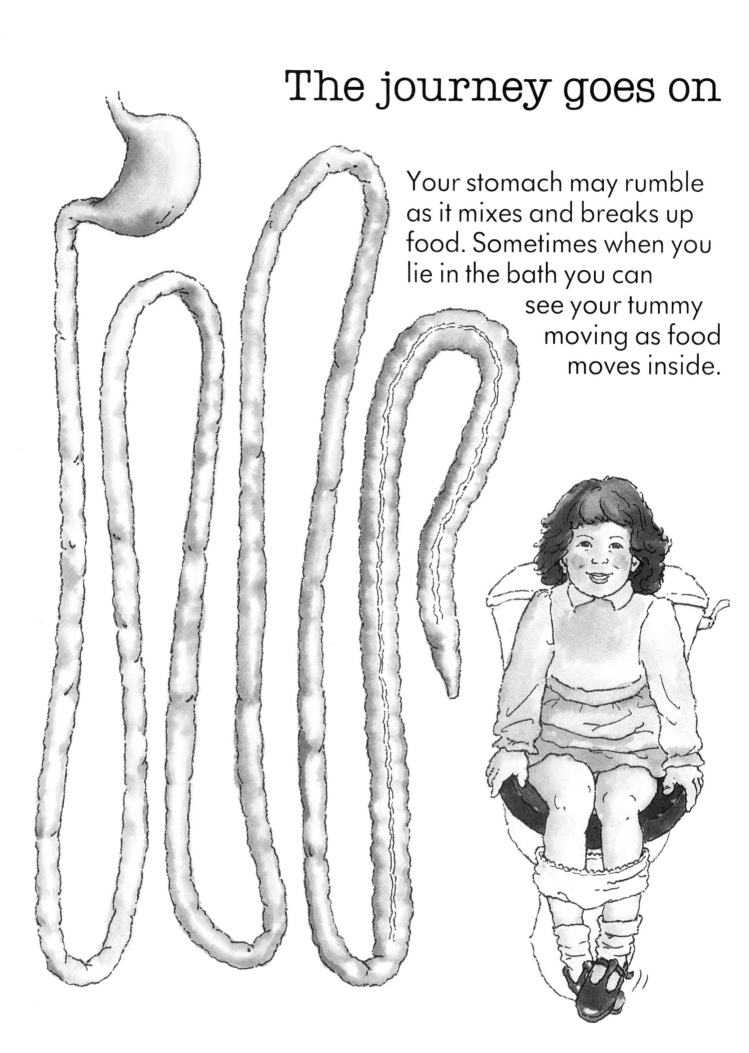

Your stomach may rumble as it mixes and breaks up food. Sometimes when you lie in the bath you can see your tummy moving as food moves inside.

After the food mixture leaves your stomach it travels on inside your gut. The gut is a very long tube which is all coiled up inside you. If you don't believe it all fits in, lift the flap. As food travels, your body sorts out the useful parts and keeps them. It keeps water too.

The parts that aren't needed carry on to the very end of the gut and come out when you go to the lavatory.

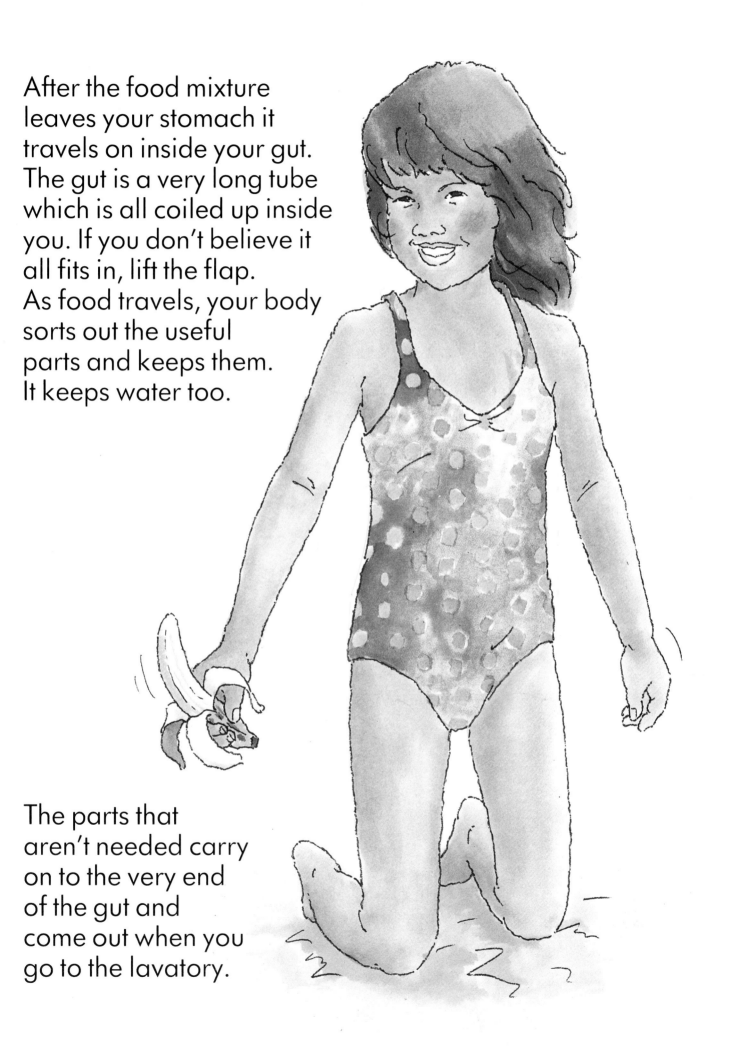

Blood

Blood helps fight germs inside your body to stop you becoming ill. It carries all sorts of things around and you need quite a lot of it. The blood in a grown up's body would fill about 15 cans and a newborn baby's blood might only fill one can.

How many cans of blood do you think you have? Count up the cans in front of the boy and you will see. Would a very small child have as many as you?

When you have a drink you are helping to keep your blood runny, which is very important. Any left-over water that your body does not need is made into pee.

The colour of blood

When you cut your skin it quickly mends itself. Red blood leaks out of the cut and dries hard to make a scab. The scab protects the new skin growing underneath. When it has mended the scab drops off.

You don't have to cut yourself to find out that blood is red. Press the tip of a fingernail gently. You can see it go white as the blood is squeezed away.

Let go and watch the blood rush back. Nails are just a kind of hard skin which protects your fingers and toes.

Blood vessels

Blood travels around your body in tubes called blood vessels. They are like tunnels, all different sizes.

Pull down your lower eyelid gently and look in a mirror. The blood vessels look like tiny red lines.

Lift the flap and you can see the biggest blood vessels in your body. Blood can move all over your body from your head down to your toes in these tubes. The biggest tubes are near your heart. They divide and divide into smaller and smaller tubes and branch out all over your body. Look at the blood vessels on the inside of your wrist. The blood in them is bluer and is going back to your heart to become fresh and red again.

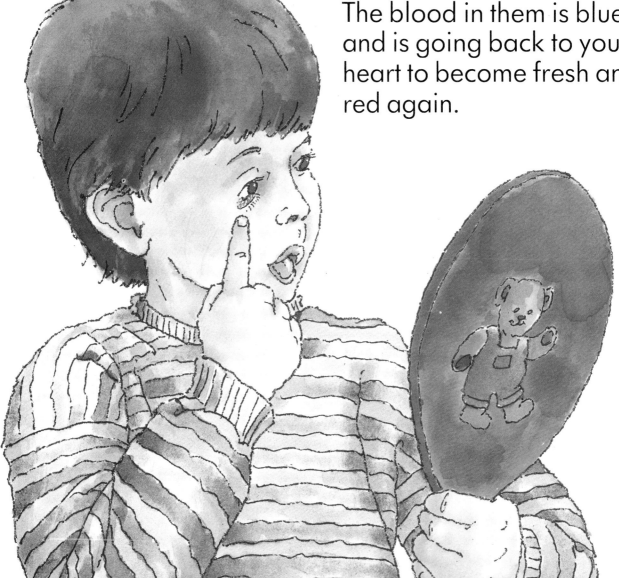

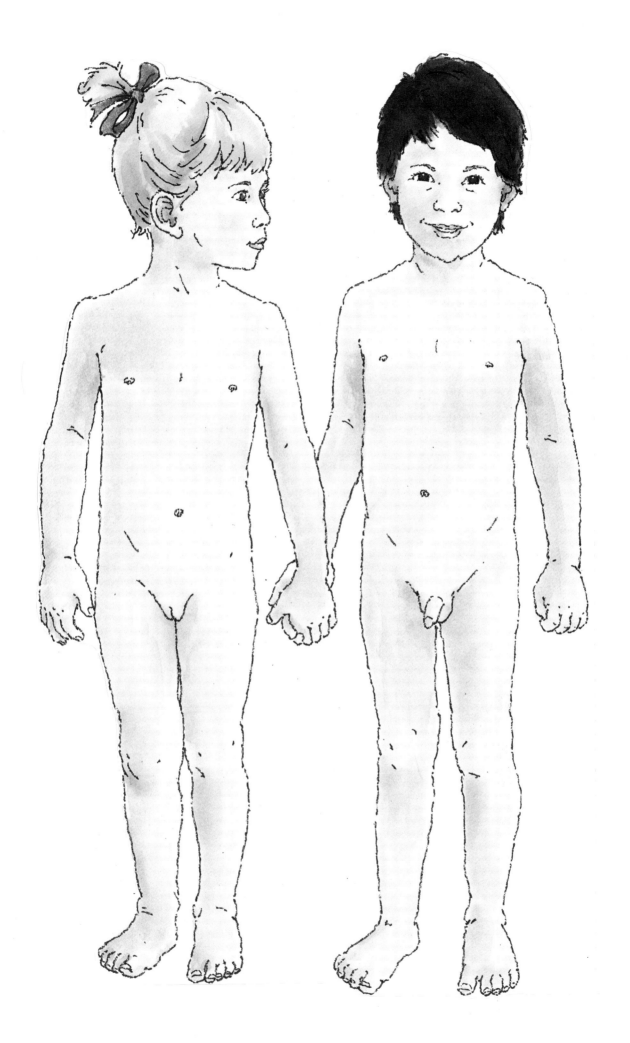

Heartbeat

Blood cannot move itself round your body. It is pushed round by your heart. Your heart is made of muscle which squeezes and when it squeezes it pushes the blood along. See for yourself how it works by filling a plastic bottle with water and putting a piece of tube on the end. When you squeeze it the water is pushed along the tube in the same way as your blood is pushed along blood vessels by the heart.

Lift the flap and see where your heart is. When the heart squeezes it makes a thumping sound.

Put your ear against someone's chest and listen to their heartbeat.

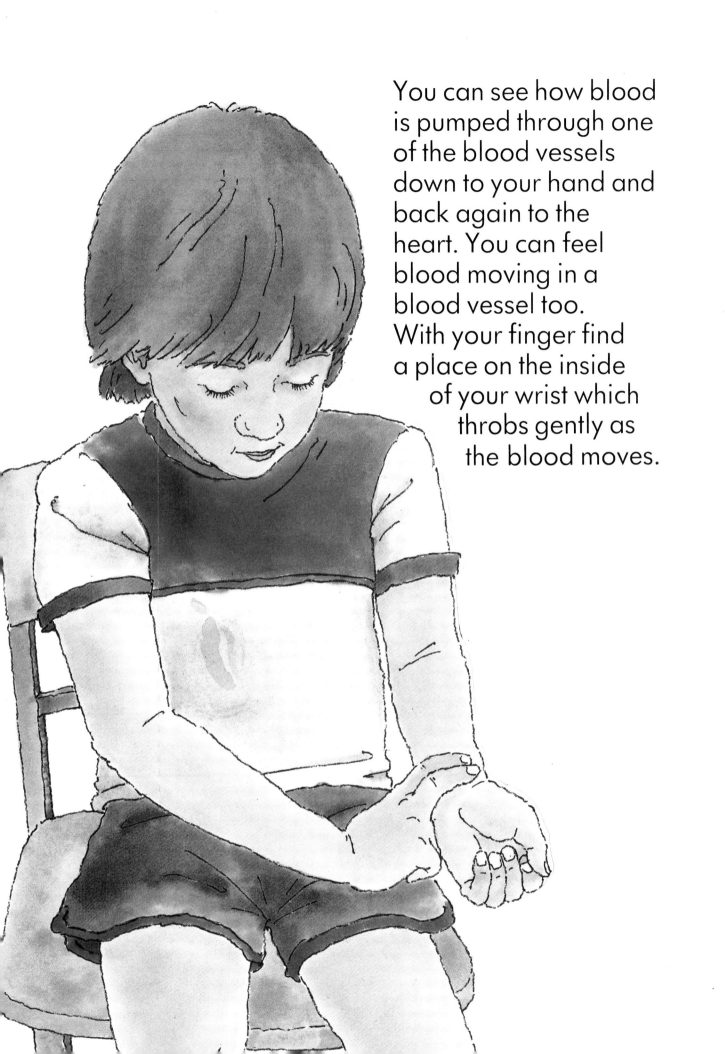

You can see how blood is pumped through one of the blood vessels down to your hand and back again to the heart. You can feel blood moving in a blood vessel too. With your finger find a place on the inside of your wrist which throbs gently as the blood moves.

What does blood do?

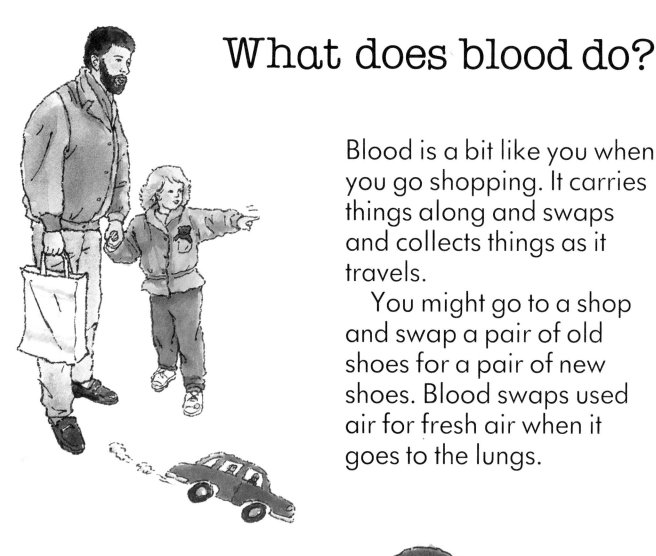

Blood is a bit like you when you go shopping. It carries things along and swaps and collects things as it travels.

You might go to a shop and swap a pair of old shoes for a pair of new shoes. Blood swaps used air for fresh air when it goes to the lungs.

Or you might go into another shop and collect something quite new, like a hat, to take home. Blood collects something new — food — when it goes near the gut. Then it carries the food back to the parts of your body that need it.

All together now

Blood doesn't take food and air to just one place. Blood delivers food and air to any part of your body which needs them. Muscles need food and air when they pull.

Make a fist and feel the muscles go hard as they pull. Everything, except bones, can bend or stretch so that when your muscles pull, your body can change shape and move. Use some more muscles to change the shape of your body. Can you find the muscles which pull your legs up when you jump? All of your body needs the food and air brought by the blood to grow bigger. Do you know how much you've grown since your last birthday?

Lift the flap and
see how everything
fits neatly together
inside you.

Here are a few more ways to explore your outside and your inside.

More about... Bones

Bones are rubbery things full of calcium salts which make them hard. Put a thin chicken bone in vinegar for a week. The vinegar takes out the hard calcium and leaves the bendy bone shape.

More about... Keeping warm and keeping cool

Your body needs to be warm to work properly so it makes its own heat. Blood carries the heat to all the parts of your body including your skin. When you feel hot, lots of blood goes to the skin. As it loses the extra warmth you cool down. Try running hard until you feel hot. All the blood coming up to your skin to cool off makes you flush. Can you remember what else your skin does to cool you down?

More about... Teeth

Some of your teeth cut food like scissors. Some of them mash food up. Do you think that your cutting teeth are the same shape as your mashing teeth? If you are not sure which is which, have a look at your teeth in a mirror or eat some food and see what they do.

More about...
Breathing

Did you know that the used air you breathe out has water in it? Breathe on to a cold mirror. It will go misty. Touch the mist and feel how wet it is.

More about...
Heartbeat

Was it hard to find your pulse at your wrist? You can feel your pulse in other places too. One place is under your jaw. Feel very gently with your fingertips. Can you feel it throbbing?

Outside In was conceived, edited and designed
by Frances Lincoln Limited
Apollo Works, 5 Charlton Kings Road, London NW5 2SB

First published in Great Britain by
Macdonald and Co. (Publishers) Ltd,
Greater London House,
Hampstead Road,
London NW1 7RX
A BPCC plc Company

British Library Cataloguing in Publication Data
Smallman, Clare
Outside In.
1. Body, Human — Juvenile Literature
I. Title
612 QP37

ISBN 0 356 11819 3

Printed and bound in Italy

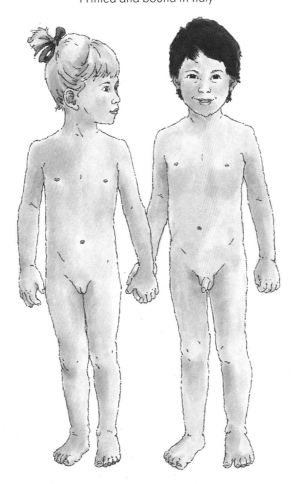

Design and Art Direction Debbie Mackinnon

Editor Pippa Rubinstein

Design Assistant Anne Wilson

Medical Adviser Dr Patricia Pearse